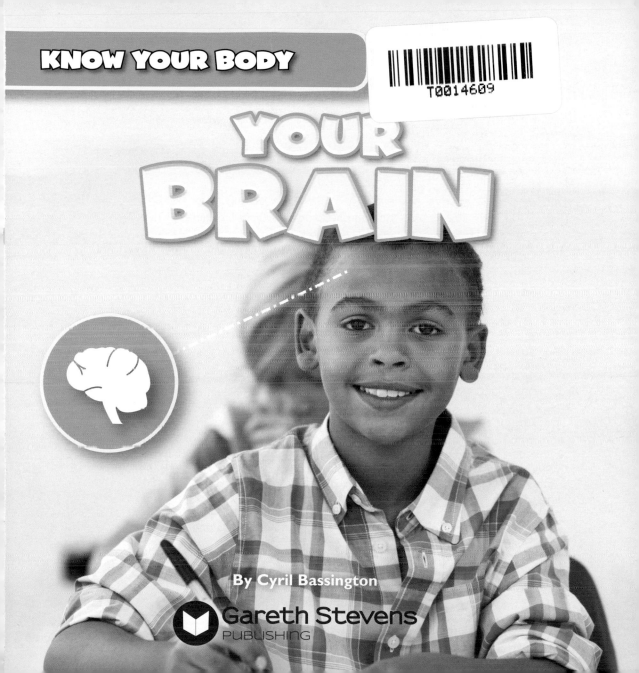

# YOUR BRAIN

By Cyril Bassington

Gareth Stevens
PUBLISHING

Please visit our website, www.garethstevens.com. For a free color catalog of all our high-quality books, call toll free 1-800-542-2595 or fax 1-877-542-2596.

Library of Congress Cataloging-in-Publication Data

Bassington, Cyril, author.
 Your brain / Cyril Bassington.
     pages cm. — (Know your body)
 Includes bibliographical references and index.
 ISBN 978-1-4824-4454-4 (pbk.)
 ISBN 978-1-4824-4398-1 (6 pack)
 ISBN 978-1-4824-4436-0 (library binding)
 1.  Brain—Juvenile literature. 2.  Human physiology—Juvenile literature.  I. Title.
 QP376.B374 2017
 612.8'2—dc23

                                        2015021476


Published in 2017 by
**Gareth Stevens Publishing**
111 East 14th Street, Suite 349
New York, NY 10003

Copyright © 2017 Gareth Stevens Publishing

Designer: Andrea Davison-Bartolotta
Editor: Therese Shea

Photo credits: Cover, p. 1 Nuestockimages/Getty Images; pp. 3, 4, 6, 8, 10, 12, 14, 16, 18, 20, 22–24 Anna Frajtova/Shutterstock.com; p. 5 SerrNovik/iStock/Thinkstock; pp. 7, 15 (inset) CLIPAREA/Shutterstock.com; p. 9 Sebastian Kaulitzki/Hemera/Thinkstock; p. 11 (main) Fotokostic/Shutterstock.com; pp. 11 (inset), 13 (inset) decade3d/ Shutterstock.com; p. 13 (main) Carlos Caetano/Shutterstock.com; p. 15 (main) Creatas Images/Creatas/Thinkstock; p. 17 (main) XiXingXing/iStock/Thinkstock; p. 17 (inset) © iStockphoto.com/Eraxion; p. 19 Image Source/Getty Images; p. 21 Cathy Yeulet/Hemera/Thinkstock.

Printed in the United States of America

CPSIA compliance information: Batch #CS16GS: For further information contact Gareth Stevens, New York, New York at 1-800-542-2595.

# CONTENTS

**Boldface** words appear in the glossary.

# In Control

When you play video games, you might use a controller. Your brain is the controller of your body. It controls your body's activities. It's where your thoughts and feelings come from. The brain is at work even when you're asleep!

5

# What Is It?

Your brain is made up of many, many **nerve** cells. It's shaped a bit like a mushroom or umbrella. Different parts of the brain have different jobs. The parts work together with other nerves in your body. Together, they're called the nervous system.

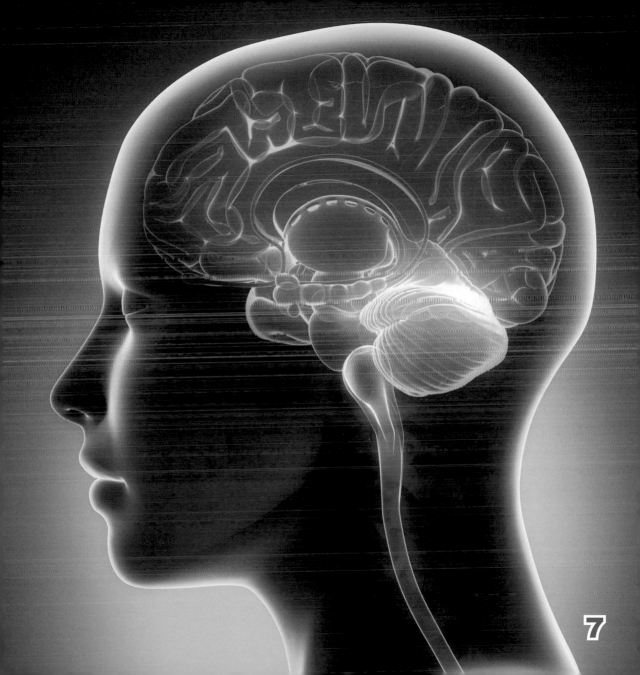

# How It Works

The brain receives messages from nerve cells in your body. It uses those messages to send orders to other body parts, such as **organs** and **muscles**. Messages can travel around the body as fast as 200 miles (322 km) per hour!

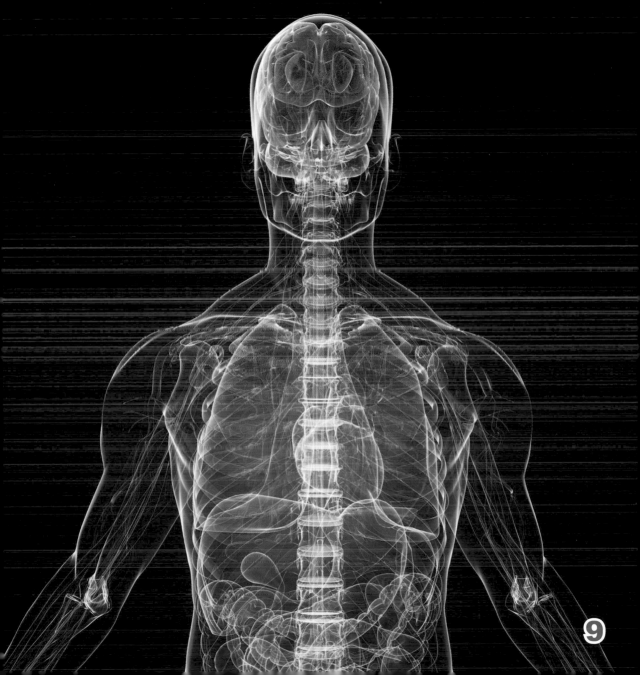

## Many Parts

Different parts of the brain have different names. The largest part, at the top, is called the cerebrum (suh-REE-bruhm). That's where you think, sense, and remember. The cerebrum also sends orders to your muscles when you want them to move.

cerebrum

11

The cerebellum (sehr-uh-BEH-luhm) is a lot smaller. It's at the back of the brain. It controls how your muscles work together. It makes sure you can stand up and not fall over! It also helps you speak.

cerebellum

13

The brain stem is under the cerebrum. It tells the body to do activities you need to stay alive, without you even thinking about it. When you breathe and when your heart beats, it's your brain stem at work.

brain stem

The pituitary (puh-TOO-uh-tehr-ee) **gland** is the size of a pea. It keeps your body growing and makes sure it has enough **energy**. The hypothalamus (hy-poh-THA-luh-muhs) controls your body's temperature. It might make you **sweat** or shiver!

hypothalamus

pituitary gland

## Keep Learning

Your brain changes every time you learn something! When you're learning an activity, practicing helps your brain cells get used to the activity so you get better at it. Think about that when you're learning a language or music.

# A Healthy Brain

Eating fish, fruits, and vegetables is a good way to keep your brain healthy. So is exercise. Scientists think it's easier for people to learn after exercising. There's a lot we don't know about the brain. But we do know it's amazing!

# GLOSSARY

**energy:** the ability to be active

**gland:** a body part that makes something needed for a bodily function

**muscle:** one of the parts of the body that allow movement

**nerve:** a part of the body that sends messages to and from the brain and allows us to feel things

**organ:** a part inside a body, such as the heart or the lungs, that performs a task

**sweat:** to produce a cooling, salty liquid on your skin when you are hot

# FOR MORE INFORMATION

## BOOKS

Burstein, John. *The Astounding Nervous System: How Does My Brain Work?* New York, NY: Crabtree Publishing, 2009.

Hewitt, Sally. *My Brain.* Laguna Hills, CA: QEB Publishing, 2008.

Spilsbury, Richard. *The Brain and Nervous System.* Chicago, IL: Heinemann Library, 2008.

## WEBSITES

**Your Amazing Brain**
*kids.nationalgeographic.com/explore/science/your-amazing-brain/*
Read more about why your brain is an amazing organ.

**Your Brain and Nervous System**
*kidshealth.org/kid/htbw/brain.html*
Find out more about the different parts of the brain.

# INDEX